THE EWART QUARTO

Gavin Ewart

Illustrated by Nicola Jennings

Hutchinson
London Melbourne Sydney Auckland Johannesburg

For Richard Boston

Hutchinson & Co. (Publishers) Ltd

An imprint of the Hutchinson Publishing Group

17–21 Conway Street, London W1P 6JD

Hutchinson Group (Australia) Pty Ltd
30–32 Cremorne Street, Richmond South, Victoria 3121
PO Box 151, Broadway, New South Wales 2007

Hutchinson Group (NZ) Ltd
32–34 View Road, PO Box 40-086, Glenfield, Auckland 10

Hutchinson Group (SA) Pty Ltd
PO Box 337, Bergvlei 2012, South Africa

First published in this collection 1984
© Gavin Ewart 1984
Illustrations © Nicola Jennings 1984

Set in VIP Palatino by
D. P. Media Limited, Hitchin, Hertfordshire

Printed and bound in Great Britain by
Anchor Brendon Ltd, Tiptree, Essex

British Library Cataloguing in Publication Data
Ewart, Gavin
  The Ewart quarto.
  I Title
  821'.914   PR6055.W3

ISBN 0 09 156071 3

Contents

*   included in *The New Ewart*
†   included in *More Little Ones*

Introduction

These are all the poems of mine that appeared in the magazine *Quarto*, under the editorship of my friend Richard Boston. Indeed, this book stands as a memorial to his enterprise. Four other friends, Peter Porter, Craig Raine, John Ryle and Carol Rumens (in chronological order) were the Poetry Editors during that periodical's lively and stimulating life.

As friends, perhaps they were insufficiently critical of the work I submitted – though I think not. Occasional verse, of the broadsheet and ballad kind, has its place in the world of literature. So do the small edged comments that are at the other end of the size scale. Three of these appeared last year in *More Little Ones*, published by Anvil Press Poetry – with whose permission they appear here again. Four longer poems are to be found in *The New Ewart*, the collection of the years 1980–82 that Hutchinson published. These seven poems are reprinted here for the sake of completeness.

I feel I ought to apologize to the ghost of Auden and to Charles Osborne, Roy Fuller, and Seamus Heaney for taking their names in vain. No serious aspersions are meant to be cast on them, or their work.

I must also thank Nicola Jennings for her stimulating illustrations.

A Pindaric Ode on the Occasion of the Third Test Match Between England and Australia, Played at Headingley, Yorkshire – 16–21 July, 1981

Well, GATTING was batting and YALLOP came in at a gallop
to save a single . . . we could mix and mingle
with the loud crowd, on our telescreens we saw the best
  match
ever to be called a Test Match . . .

Don't be abrupt, don't interrupt,
just keep quiet, don't riot, sit still and listen,
hear the Umpires' bell – I'm ready to tell
a story of glory and the unfading laurel crowns that
  glisten . . .

THURSDAY
Australia went in first, they were soon grinding away on a
  day
when England were finding it hard. I tell you, mate,
the English bowlers didn't bowl very straight,
it was like watching a coffee-grinder or standing behind a
cement-mixer, as those batsmen went through the motions,
they knew they had oceans of time. Their slowness was a
  crime
and didn't produce standing ovations – but justified,
buildings don't stand up without foundations . . .

FRIDAY
203 for 3, and a catch dropped by GOWER, the power
and the glory seemed as though it had really deserted
  BREARLEY.
OLD bowled quite well; but all this day
the Australians seemed well on their way.
DYSON didn't charge at the ball like a bison;
but he made 102, and 102s, like the 89 made by HUGHES,
and YALLOP's 58, mean a good score – and a lot more.
  Confidence.

9

They declared at 9 for 401 – for England not much fun,
though BOTHAM bowled straight and moved the ball both
  early and late,
the one ray of light in the gloom (6 for 95). Still, England's
  doom
could be seen to loom. BOTHAM seemed to prove it –
if he could swing it, the Australians too would certainly move
  it,
by seam and flight.
But no untoward fright. No English wicket fell that night.

SATURDAY
Yet England didn't rise again on that third day.
GOOCH out for 2. The thing to do seemed to be to mooch
around, BOYCOTT 12, BREARLEY 10, even GOWER
only very briefly came into flower.
24. Again some light from BOTHAM – where others were
  thrifty
he was prodigal, with a well-struck 50.
LILLEE, ALDERMAN, LAWSON bowled well – at the stumps.
Far better than the English bowlers. A bad night, with
  grinding molars
and all England's supporters down in the dumps.

MONDAY
England 174 all out and, following on,
GOOCH, with the score at zero, had already gone.
The radio mentioned odds of 500 to 1
for an England win. But this wasn't the Oval, there weren't
  any LAKERS,
and, with regard to these odds, there can't have been many
  takers.
Would Australia even have to bat again?
The most sensible thing seemed to be to pray for rain.

227 to avoid the innings defeat.
BOYCOTT played straight, calm and unflappable (46),
some of WILLEY's more aggressive strokes (33) were very
　　clappable.
But 4 down for 41! Even 5 for 105,
there didn't seem much to keep our hopes alive.
It was like the tide inexorably flooding in over the sand,
seven wickets had gone for 135. No sign of a stand,
like King Canute, nobody could send the sea back with a
　　cricket boot,
92 runs still needed for Australia to bat again, the steep hill of
　　the follow-on
and only three wickets left,
any English laugh must have been a hollow one!

But BOTHAM, looking like a lion on a British egg,
seemed to be willing to have a brief, glorious thrash,
pulling, driving, cutting and sweeping to leg,
with (once) something not much different from a tennis
　　overhead smash . . .

and, slowly but surely, we realized that he knew what he was
　　doing
and although it was very clear that he was riding his luck
the ball met the meat of the bat, this wasn't just cause for
　　booing
or irresponsible (like the slogger who's out for a duck).

The next day's papers compared him to
that six-hitting fabulous Croucher, Jessop –
and indeed he jumped down the pitch like a gressop
(the Old English for what James Joyce with his Irish voice
　　called a gracehoper

11

and most ordinary people call a grasshopper).
One particular six, a tremendous one, parabola-tall,
made one feel pretty sorry for the ball.

DILLEY, too, turned aggressive. 56 runs, and all made with
    style.
Someone shouted 'Why didn't you bowl like that?'
He was out at 252. A century partnership.
The Australian bowlers, even LILLEE, began to look
    ordinary.
BOTHAM's hundred. BREARLEY gave him the *stay there!*
    signal, very clearly.
From then on he shielded OLD, running singles at the ends of
    overs
and scoring in fours only (twos were difficult).
OLD was bowled for 29, a good innings.
Then it was WILLIS. 351 for nine
at close of play. Fine. A commentator was heard to say:
'They need a hundred runs to bowl at!' These they had.
It still looked hopeless, but not quite so bad.

TUESDAY
BOTHAM hit one more four, ALDERMAN got WILLIS.
356 all out. When they went in
Australia needed only 130 to win.
It all went quietly ahead, though BOTHAM got WOOD for ten.
DYSON and CHAPPELL looked as firm as rocks, and then
DILLEY went off to have a boot repaired. WILLIS took over –
and from then on the Australian batsmen were never in
    clover.
That wild Goose flew in like a bat out of Hell –
3 wickets in 11 balls, without a run being scored!
Surely the batsmen to come must have prayed to the Lord!
CHAPPELL, HUGHES and YALLOP – the names say it all.

12

This was the kind of bowling you can't play at all!
OLD had BORDER for a duck. MARSH didn't have BOTHAM's
    luck
and DILLEY boundary-caught him at fine leg, one of the
    hardest blows struck.
Before that DYSON went. 68 for 6. Soon just 75 for 8.
Only LILLEE at the end, with BRIGHT, showed any kind of
    fight.
BRIGHT 19, LILLEE 17 (DYSON made 34
and this was very easily the top score).
55 runs needed. Two wickets to fall.
WILLIS had LILLEE caught by GATTING, a mishit hook off a
    less straight ball.

BREARLEY said afterwards, in a sort of magnificat,
'I didn't think WILLIS could still bowl like that.'

BOTHAM came back. OLD dropped ALDERMAN twice in an
    over.
If that had been FLETCHER
that Yorkshire Chauvinist crowd would have made a meal of
    it, you betcher
life, as one of the commentators said.
Still, though everyone was tense, under his beard OLD's face
    must have been a bit red . . .

Finally, though, WILLIS knocked out BRIGHT's middle
    stump,
and everyone jumped for joy, a really unbelievable jump!
111 all out. They'd done it by 18 runs . . .

And this is an ode to Cricket, Cricket and its white-robed
    sons!
Like the bounce of a rugger ball, you can't tell which way it'll
    go,
it's totally unpredictable, if it's like anything at all
it's truly like a game of soccer played with a rugger ball!
But of course you must praise WILLIS (8 for 43)
and BOTHAM's magnificent innings – 149 not out.
Goose and Guy the Gorilla
were the two favourite flavours, like (say) Strawberry and
    Vanilla –
but MIKE BREARLEY also deserves praise,
as a first-class Captain in a good many different ways.

This tribute that mangles the epic and the lyric,
this rough populist Pindaric panegyric,
this dithyrambic doggerel is here to make the claim
that since STODDARD did it in Sydney in 1894
no other Test side in history has ever followed on and still
    won the game!

On the 100th Birthday of
P.G.Wodehouse

(15 October 1981, also the Centenary of the Chinese poet Lu Xun)

Like most of us (Time's temple's architrave)
he spends his hundredth birthday in the grave
(the squiggly bits in architecture, we
are not important to Eternity)
but here was something, happy to be 'light',
that shines like Shakespeare, just as bravely bright!

The words that cozen us, the ancient ploys!
The fairy-story worlds – where girls and boys
face aunts and alienists, the dragon seed,
and ritual attire (without, they bleed)
must save them (ties! oh, ties! oh, waistcoats, spats!)
and sweet flat-chested girls in floppy hats!
Where love is love, without its sexy smell,
and there's no stroking at the bearded well.

It's true the working class, the vast majorities,
and women in their sharp oppressed sororities,
don't ever find him really all that funny.
Perhaps to dig him much, you must have money?

Even war's spillage, its seepage and its ullage,
didn't much disturb his dreams of Dulwich
(there's not much doubt that his idea of heaven
was just to watch the Dulwich First Eleven).
He kept his innocence, exploited when
the Nazis said they too were gentlemen.
O'Casey called him a performing flea,
there to amuse applauding bourgeoisie –
quite right. But more, much more, to it than that!
He only understood one kind of bat.
The Draculas of politics flew by,
he hardly knew that they were in the sky.

Perhaps he was to blame – he should have known –
a good man, without malice, on his own
he much increased the gaiety of nations
by serving Art with daily ministrations,
as much as Wilde's or Yeats's, Seamus Heaney's . . .

Lounge lizards have a bifurcated penis
(but did I know what people did in bed?)
one of my father's (medical) students said –
a joke I treasured (at the age of ten) –
I was well into Wodehouse, even then.
No, surely I was older, more like twelve?
Walt Whitmanlike, I contradict myself –
I take the books down – 1928!
But still a sexless pre-pubertal state.
Leave It To Psmith, A Damsel In Distress,
Ukridge, the Mulliners, *Money For Nothing*, yes,
beans, crumpets, Jeeves, a soulful poetess . . .
On those foxed pages and the thoughts they house
I was well sluiced and quite content to browse!

Before him, Richmal Crompton filled my shelves –
two first-class writers, a class by themselves
(Doyle, Haggard, Henty, Westerman and Wells
had no more humour than *The Book of Kells*).

But what makes Wodehouse leader by a mile
isn't his thought but his pellucid style,
clear and colloquial. The thought (and lots)
went into all those complicated plots,
worked out like early musical comedies.
Reality? Oh, no! far from it! Is
there any backtrack, short cut, sideways twist
that labyrinthine Wodehouse ever missed?

Those characters more addictive than the bottle!
Gussie (newt-fancier), the young Fink-Nottle.
Lord Emsworth, Tuppy Glossop, Bertie Wooster,
even Aunt Agatha's a morale-booster!
Anatole ('God's gift to the gastric juices'),
Percy Pilbeam, Chimp Twist, both foul abuses,
snakes in the grass, whose moral turpitude
would make a moralist throw up – or burp (it would!),
Rosie M. Banks and martyred Bingo Little,
the forceful female and the male, more brittle . . .

Duet for Aunt and Nephew. Critics say
each novel is a musicless musical play.
I'd go along with that. But still the story
isn't exactly his great crowning glory –
we know the Efficient Baxter will retreat
and dithering Lord Emsworth find his feet,
all Aunts be foiled, and True Love find a way,
Jeeves work his magic, for ever and a day
the steel-willed girls will have their silly asses,
with not much mention of the toiling masses
(O'Casey, down!). Blandings is Eden. Waugh
was right too. This is Alice's door.
Soon lost forever, Innocence is the key
to Never Never Lands where all are free
in pastoral joy – a humorous Brideshead
(nostalgia for childhood, not wine and bed).

He has his century. Now clap him in!
And send Sir Roderick Glossop howling to the bin!

And Art A Ruminant

'but wonder
If in fact art is better than life.'
ROY FULLER: *Bagatelles*

Strange that I still a parlous chorus croak,
Alarmingly at variance with art!
Curious the enormous distance that the heart
Must cover in some worn old buffer's joke,

How now I must fumble what I once could poke –
The Muse's groin, she being a bright young tart
(Strange that!). I still a parlous chorus croak.
Alarmingly at variance with art,

How odd that she should sip her vesper coke
And that her gaze, as one feared from the start,
Should pierce us, eye a veritable dart
Thrown in a pub by some young beer-loud bloke!
Strange! That I still a parlous chorus croak!

Auden

Photographed, he looked like Spencer Tracy
or even Danny Kaye –
in the late Forties. But later it was wiser
to look the other way.

A Bit Of A Ballad

Scotland v. Australia, Murrayfield, 18 December 1981

Oh, broken, broken was the play!
And blawn the half-time whistle!
The Wallabies hae scored tries three,
Four penalties the Thistle.

The second half now gars begin,
On the snaw-stripit green,
And but twelve points the braw Scots hae,
The Wallabies fifteen.

But 'tis the bonny Andy Irvine
That kicks the penalty
That levels a', 15-15,
As level as your e'e.

And they hae ta'en the whisky malt
That stand to see the battle,
And syne they harry the Scottish team,
As drovers harry cattle!

The lions on the standards roar,
And Scotland scores again!
'Tis the muckle Rutherford—
A drappit goal, ye may ken!

'Hauld fast! Hauld fast!' Clerk Irvine cries,
'My bonny lads, wi' me!
We'll weill withstand, on either hand,
The assaults o' the enemie!'

The Wallabies are ravenous,
They sling the ba' aboot—
The Scots defence stands firm as rock,
They dinna care a hoot!

There's but five minutes' playing time,
Australians leap and rin,
And 'tis gowd jerseys everywhere,
Like a rugby loony-bin!

But 'tis the muckle Rutherford
Has ta'en the ba' in's hands
And kicked it full high i' the freezing air
And higher than the stands.

The ba' has landed on its point,
The ba' has bounced full high –
And 'tis the wee Renwick has caught it and
'Tis an inescapable try!

Oh, wae, wae, were the Wallabies,
Baith here and owre the faem,
Tae see the braw wee Renwick rin
And bear the victory hame!

For now 'tis 15-22 –
Australia does trail,
A score that hurts. Irvine converts,
Like driving in a nail!

And so rejoice in Embro toun,
The final whistle blaws,
Mak merrie, 24-15!
All Scots, they hae guid cause!

The Phantom of the Opera

In a world full of Thomas Hardy-type ironies
what could be properer
than that a Literature Director should be
a man who only cares about music –
Charles Osborne,
the phantom of the opera.

Contemporaries

Well, to begin with, you must know
Shakespeare was called an 'Upstart Crow' . . .
and now we find from poets' letters
what they thought of bardic betters.

Graves liked Lawrence (mad T.E.).
D.H. (a poet too if he
wasn't so obsessed with sex!)
sent no current through his flex.
Graves, an engine in a siding –
shunted there by Laura Riding –
thought all Auden's verse was 'fake'
and Willie Yeats a big mistake.
He loved Skelton and E. Rumming's
tunnings – and (save us!) e.e.cummings!
Pound was crazy, vain though vital,
no poet – hadn't earned the title.

Another part of that same wood:
and here, too, things are not so good,
Professor Lucas, no wild zealot,
calls Eliot a 'drunken helot',
D.H. calls Joyce *'Olla podrida'*
(a putrid cabbage, yes, dear reader!),
while V. Woolf thinks him middle class
or lower, and G. Stein, alas!,
knows she's more 'advanced' than him
(though Stan supports his brother Jim).
Wyndham Lewis (first name Percy)
sternly watches, without mercy,
what a crew without a cox!
Hemingway – a big 'dumb ox',
Virginia too, he says, somehow,
is less a woman than a cow!

And all the while the *famille* Sitwell
goes for the foes whose throats would slit well –
does it get better, does it worsen?
Edith calls Enright (D), 'a person',
while Geoffrey Grigson causes pain
by naming *her* as 'that Old Jane'
and shouting loud, without duplicity,
that she's an expert at publicity!
And Spender: 'Who *is* Peter Porter?'
Campbell, reactionary snorter,
whose afternoon's a Fascist faun day,
attacks the Leftist team, Macspaunday.

(But Byron, once, recall, gave Wordsworth
a most unpleasant nickname: Turdsworth.
Romanticised and Jeffrey Farnol'd,
Shelley was called by Matthew Arnold
an 'angel', yes, but 'ineffectual',
and Aldous too, that intellectual,
flew mothlike from a Bloomsbury rug
to put him down – a 'fat white slug'.)

And so, we know, the bad opinions,
throughout Her Majesty's Dominions
and places where she holds no sway
like the big-headed U.S.A.,
are even now being written down –
this moment as a clot or clown
you and I are being described
in private letters, diatribed
outspokenly (no halfway hints)
in all the highbrow public prints,
but most of all, by butch and camp,
firmly thumbed down with a stamp!

27

On Being Asked by My Daughter to Lend Her My Father's Leather Motoring Coat of 1930

No, no, I couldn't! Not for an hour or a minute!
Dan would be off on his motorbike, straightaway, in it!
It would very quickly be covered in grease or oil —
the very things that most incontestably spoil
a coat of such a kind, a genuine collector's piece
but most vulnerable (as McGonagall would have said) to oil
   and grease!

In fact, most of Evelyn Waugh's highborn friends had coats
   like that;
they came to them naturally, like cream to a prize cat.

Or, if you wore it, with its true soft leather feel, it
wouldn't be long before your local criminals set out to steal it.
Because a real leather coat, buttoning to the neck,
with a broad leather belt (suitable now for a discotheque),
was Hitler's Choice in 1938, the year when the Czech
was sold down the river by a Conservative regime
that thought itself (they all do) the cream of the cream.

So I must refuse. And if you ever see
that coat walking around, inside it will be *me!*

Sonnet: The Hymn-Singers

We're officer cadets in 1940 –
and some of us won't get out of this war alive.
There's snow, and ice, on the gun park. With freezing hands
we bring the gun into action (so many seconds flat).
Later, in pubs, we sing the rugger songs,
establishing the warmth of wartime, camaraderie,
like women's sewing bees, one sex together,
making a joke of love we're frightened of . . .

Years later will come the impotent polymaths
to say we shouldn't have sung them. Though very young
   men
think women and battle are equally tests, they'll say
it's homosexual. But we were a Congregation,
hymn-singing in that darkness – so would you!
Those sex-linked Spartans knew a thing or two!

And Female Smells in Shuttered Rooms

Short square fingers stuffing pipes
and Kilpeck witches in the streets,
all the Apeneck Sweeney types
riding women, staining sheets!

Sensitives wince into the world,
it seems to them so rough and coarse,
French poets, filigreed and pearled,
are better than a wingèd horse

and perfumes floating round an arm
than the crude odours of the groin –
foul Circe with her porcine charm
and Charon with his deadly coin!

Once, Eliot, I was shy as you
and impotent as you (I guess);
I failed at what I tried to do,
my sex-life was an awful mess.

But Stephen, Wystan, Christopher
enjoyed themselves with loads of boys,
they did not hesitate, demur,
or shrink from treating them like toys.

The lad is sad who masturbates.
It's good but not quite good enough –
though (once) was good enough for Yeats.
The wet warmth of that furry muff,

the girlish kiss, attracted still,
tiptilted tits, the big-eyed gaze –
I ended feeling rather ill;
I missed my homosexual phase.

31

A forest, round about, of cocks
grew up, a sexual Sacred Wood,
to flaunt Eternity, mock clocks;
and there, alone, I weeping stood.

Those others kicked the gong around –
Tom, Dick (especially Dick) and Harry
gave them the bliss I never found.
They even took time off to marry.

A nightmare (you could call it) and
the worse because I was so young –
Love seemed a Never Never Land.
Like Keats, infected in the lung,

I yearned for Light that never was
(there's not much fun in lonely yearning)
and this was made much worse because
I wasn't in a job and earning.

So, unemployed and unenjoyed,
I sipped my bitter, loveless cup –
until, like Fathers out of Freud,
the bloody Army took me up!

Love Song

As you get old you begin to wonder –
what was all that lightning and thunder
actually about?
It was more than holding hands,
it had a lot to do with glands –
but now you're far out,

floating calmly in a lonely seascape;
passionate rose-garden, stormed treescape
very long ago
left behind – what they call Youth
seems now ridiculous, uncouth
(if you want to know).

As you settle into peace, or dourness,
that bitter-sweet, that sweet-and-sourness,
is a vanished taste;
yet those who never clasped and kissed
don't know exactly what they missed
or what exactly went to waste.

Haiku: the Wit and Wisdom of Cyril Connolly

Connolly called the
British 'sheep with a nasty
side'. How very true!

Haiku: Locomotor Ataxia

Four steps. A long halt.
The old man has a poet's
bad creative block.

The Locative

'The Locative. The names of towns, small islands,
domus, humus and *rus*.' *Kennedy's Latin Primer*

The names of towns are so evocative
they have to go into the locative –
Pompeiis, Adelstrops and Selbournes,
full of the peasants and the well-borns,
where the curates had misgivings
about exchanging rural livings.
Small islands? Procida or Ischia –
Latin freedom was much friskier,
at home on that volcanic soil
(Ibsen and Auden on the boil),
no birth control – sex too was rural,
a tergo, interruptus, intercrural!

Seamus Heaney

He's very popular with his mates.
I think I'm Auden, he thinks he's Yeats.

New! (a Pam Ayres)

It was the Fourth of January,
The New Year was very new!
I got on the train at Putney,
To take me to Waterloo,

I had to hop on quickly –
British Rail won't wait –
Seven in the compartment,
I was number eight.

I settled in the one empty seat,
Me basket on me lap.
On me right was a woman,
On me left was a chap.

I saw how he held his paper
And glanced now and then at his feet –
The news was less new than his shoes were,
My, they shone bright and neat!

The woman on me other side
Cradled a shiny bag,
Dusted the black patent leather,
As new as a store's price tag!

Opposite me was a fellow,
And there at his feet on the floor
Was a beautiful newborn briefcase,
Set there for all to adore!

Accidentally I'd kicked it
As I struggled onto the train,
He looked as though he could kill me –
then kill me all over again!

On his right was another man,
A wine-coloured scarf round his neck,
New and noticeable – there he sat,
As proud as Gregory Peck!

Three in a row, on his right again,
An umbrella man sat erect,
Twirling a new umbrella,
Superior and select!

Upright and perfect between his feet,
He leaned on it like a sword,
Like a symbol of knighthood,
Well-bred and just a bit bored.

Away to me left a woman sat,
Next to the lad with the shoes;
A pair of gloves lay in her lap,
Uncreased, with no sign of use.

From time to time she stroked them.
It was like shouting aloud,
She and the others, how Santa
Had certainly done them proud!

But there was a seventh person,
Next to the briefcase man –
He sat there wedged in his corner,
Pale and haggard and wan.

From his feet up, he was shabby,
Worn shoes and a cuff-frayed shirt,
Nothing of his was smooth and clean,
He looked rough and acquainted with dirt.

41

He truly did look scruffy,
There by the NO SMOKING sign.
He had nothing new about him
That I could guess or divine!

I saw he was frantically chewing,
He had a brown-stained right hand,
And as I looked for *his* newness
I began to understand!

He'd made a New Year Resolution,
And one that isn't a joke!
What was new with him was his new resolve
Never again to smoke!

This poem is based entirely, in every detail, on
a journey made by my wife – an example of the
poet using another person's experience as his
raw material.

The Most Famous Poem of
J. Strugnell

Say not the Strugnell nought availeth,
  The biro and the beer are vain,
Poetic craft wherein he baileth
  Lost on the vast illit'rate main!

If odes are dupes, verse plays are liars,
  Where meaning lies in tropes concealed,
The High Sublime is looking pious
  And something silly is revealed.

For while the poets, proudly reading,
  Don't entice the prettiest girls,
Faber and Faber, both, are speeding
  To smother them in gold and pearls.

And not by magazine sales only
  Or playing trumpets, all that jazz,
Shall Strugnell cease from feeling lonely –
  Slim volumes give him what he has!

Jubilate Matteo

For I rejoice in my cat Matty.

For his coat is variegated in black and brown, with white undersides.

For in every way his whiskers are marvellous.

For he resists the Devil and is completely neuter.

For he sleeps and washes himself and walks warily in the ways of Putney.

For he is at home in the whole district of SW15.

For in this district the great Yorkshire Murderer ate his last meal before he entered into captivity.

For in the Book of Crime there is no name like John Reginald Halliday Christie.

For Yorkshire indeed excels in all things, as Geoffrey Boycott is the best Batsman.

For the Yorkshire Ripper and the Hull Arsonist have their horns exalted in glory.

For Yorkshire is therefore acknowledged the greatest county.

For Hull was once of the company, that is now of Humberside.

For Sir Leonard Hutton once scored 364 runs in a Test Match.

For Fred Trueman too is a flagrant glory to Yorkshire.

For my cat wanders in the ways of the angels of Yorkshire.

For in his soul God has shown him a remarkable vision of Putney.

For he has also trodden in the paths of the newly fashionable.

For those who live in Gwendolen Avenue cry 'Drop dead, darling!'

For in Cambalt Road and Dealtry Road where the Vet lives there are professional people.

For Erpingham Road and Danemere Street and Dryburgh Road include the intelligentsia.

For in Clarendon Drive the British Broadcasting Corporation is rampant.

For the glory of God has deserted the simple.

For the old who gossiped in Bangalore Road are unknown to the dayspring.

For there is a shortage of the old people who adorned the novels of William Trevor.

For in the knowledge of this I cling to the old folkways of Gwalior Road and Olivette Street.

For I rejoice in my cat, who has the true spirit of Putney.

The Beginning of an Ode on
Who's Who

I'm terribly excited –
I have been invited
to join that great bunch of nonentities
who have the inflated identities,
such as Lord Leatherhead and Viscount Foxford
(who knew all the right – or were they the wrong? –
people at Oxford),

metallurgists, musicians,
phenomenologists, physicians
(and almost anyone in Debrett is
sure to be in with the celebrities –
but it's not so common for the neglected scribbler
to get into this exclusive club before he's senile
or a dribbler);

though there you might someday find it,
when you were halt, lame and blinded,
your name – is it really a good dropping one?
Though once one's in there's no stopping one,
one can drawl, like MacBeth*, 'Oh course I'm in *Who's Who*
   now,'
one's poetic specific gravity is certainly multiplied
by more than two now!

I'll be there with the great ones,
the truly honoured-by-the-State ones,
in that Never-Never-Land fathers
never reached (though both my grandfathers),
with conservative academics, donnish and prudish;
among the old women of both sexes my name may seem
a tiny bit rudish?

But the military, the Naval, the flying
(who don't mind people dying),
the Earls and the epistemologists,
the dentists, divines and Catholic apologists,
those who in stately homes discuss a *cru* or a crumpet,
though they won't like it at all, I'm sure, will just
have to lump it!

* It may seem that George MacBeth has been unfairly singled out. Indeed I
could equally well have used the names of any of the included poets: Dannie
Abse, A. Alvarez, Kingsley Amis, George Barker, Patricia Beer, Sir John
Betjeman, George Mackay Brown, Charles Causley, Robert Conquest, Patric
Dickinson, Ronald Duncan, Lawrence Durrell, Sir William Empson, D. J.
Enright, Roy Fuller, Robert Gittings, Geoffrey Grigson, Thomas William
(Thom) Gunn, Ian Hamilton, Seamus Heaney, John Heath-Stubbs, Geoffrey
Hill, David Holbrook, Ted Hughes, Clive James, Elizabeth Jennings, Thomas
Kinsella, James Kirkup, Philip Larkin, Laurie Lee, John Lehmann. Peter Levi,
Christopher Logue, (George MacBeth), Norman MacCaig, Adrian Mitchell,
Kathleen Nott, Harold Pinter, Ruth Pitter, Peter Porter, Kathleen Raine,
Peter Redgrove, Henry Reed, Anne Ridler, Alan Ross, Howard Sergeant,
Penelope Shuttle, Jon Silkin, Stephen Spender, Julian Symons,
R. S. Thomas, Anthony Thwaite, Charles Tomlinson, John Wain, Sir John
Waller.
    These are all there, with Rev. Canaan Sodindo Banana (President of
Zimbabwe), Leonid Ilyich Brezhnev, the Brodie of Brodie, Barbara Cartland
(with a list of novels as long as your arm) and Sir Walter Scott (twice). Wot,
no Tambimuttu? No David Gascoyne? No (separate) Lady Wilson?